Nature Guide
URBAN WILDLIFE

CATHERINE BRERETON

Illustrated by
KATE McLELLAND

BLOOMSBURY
CHILDREN'S BOOKS
LONDON OXFORD NEW YORK NEW DELHI SYDNEY

For Liz, thank you for your company
on hundreds of urban nature walks x – C.B.

For Auntie Em, our urban explorer x – K.M.

BLOOMSBURY CHILDREN'S BOOKS
Bloomsbury Publishing Plc
50 Bedford Square, London, WC1B 3DP, UK
Bloomsbury Publishing Ireland Limited
29 Earlsfort Terrace, Dublin 2, D02 AY28, Ireland

BLOOMSBURY, BLOOMSBURY CHILDREN'S BOOKS and the Diana logo are
trademarks of Bloomsbury Publishing Plc

First published in Great Britain 2026 by Bloomsbury Publishing Plc

Text copyright © Bloomsbury Publishing Plc, 2026
Illustrations copyright © Kate McLelland, 2026
Text by Catherine Brereton

All rights reserved. No part of this publication may be: i) reproduced or transmitted
in any form, electronic or mechanical, including photocopying, recording or by
means of any information storage or retrieval system without prior permission in
writing from the publishers; or ii) used or reproduced in any way for the training,
development or operation of artificial intelligence (AI) technologies, including
generative AI technologies. The rights holders expressly reserve this publication from
the text and data mining exception as per Article 4(3) of the Digital Single Market
Directive (EU) 2019/790

A catalogue record for this book is available from the British Library

ISBN: PB: 978-1-5266-9227-6; eBook: 978-1-5266-9226-9

2 4 6 8 10 9 7 5 3 1

Printed and bound in China by Toppan Leefung Printing, DongGuan, GuangDong

To find out more about our authors and books visit
www.bloomsbury.com and sign up for our newsletters

For product safety related questions
contact productsafety@bloomsbury.com

CONTENTS

Wildlife is everywhere!	4
Wildlife-watching through the year	6
Habitats	7
What to look out for	8
How to use this book	13
Nature guide section	14
Birds	14
Mammals	34
Amphibians	46
Reptiles	50
Fish	52
Minibeasts	56
Trees	72
Flowers and other plants	78
Fungi	84
Get involved with wildlife	86
Glossary	92
Urban wildlife checklist	94

WILDLIFE IS EVERYWHERE!

In a town or city, busy with traffic and crowded with buildings, you might not expect to see wildlife. But, if you look closely, there are all sorts of living things thriving in bustling urban areas, no matter where you are or the time of year.

You can see wildlife in a garden, street or local park, along a river or canal, on the verges next to roads or from the window of a train. There are animals and plants in squares, on pavements or even on the tops of buildings. To find them, you just need a bit of practice and patience.

This book will help you recognise and learn about the wildlife you might see in towns and cities. There's so much out there to discover!

What is wildlife?

Wildlife is any living thing that is found in the wild. It includes animals, from large deer to tiny ladybirds; plants, from the tallest trees to smallest wildflowers; and fungi, which are not animals or plants. There is wildlife on land, in the sky and in the water. There are some living things around us that we don't class as wildlife: domestic pets, farm animals, animals in zoos, garden plants — and us!

Wildlife and the environment

You can find wildlife everywhere, but get to know a particular wildlife spot and you'll find out that it's special. Each green space will have its own characteristics and a unique mix of animals and plants that live and grow there.

The different types of wildlife in a place all depend on each other. Just one tree might help thousands of animal species to survive by providing food, shelter or a place to nest and perch!

Wildlife-watcher rules

- When you're watching wildlife, remember to respect it. Try to be quiet and still.

- You might be able to handle some small animals such as minibeasts, but never harm or frighten animals, and don't destroy or pick plants.

- When you are out exploring, take a trusted adult with you and pay attention to your surroundings. Stick to public paths and trails, be aware of potential hazards and do not wander onto privately owned land without permission.

Why not keep a wildlife diary? Make sure to note down every plant or animal you see, and when and where you saw it.

WILDLIFE-WATCHING THROUGH THE YEAR

Wildlife changes with the seasons — there are lots of different plants and animals to spot. Even the same creatures you see every day are getting up to different things. There's always something fun to discover!

In spring

- Try spotting birds as they gather twigs to build their nests.
- See spring flowers appearing and leaves opening on trees.
- Search for frogspawn in park ponds. Watch the tadpoles grow more and more each time you visit.

In summer

- Count how many different bees and butterflies you can spot.
- Look out for beetles, dragonflies and hoverflies too.
- If you're lucky, you might see bats on warm summer evenings.

In autumn

- Enjoy spectacular leaf displays as many trees change colour in autumn.
- Watch for squirrels burying acorns.
- Search for fungi popping up all over woods and parks.

In winter

- Watch birds visiting feeders, which will be busier in winter when there is less natural food around.
- See winter berries on trees, such as holly and hawthorn.
- Look out for animal tracks, especially in the snow.

HABITATS

A place where an animal or plant lives is called its habitat. The right habitat will provide the right types of food as well as places to shelter and to have babies. For a plant, the right habitat will have the right kind of soil, the right amount of light or shade and water. Even within a town or city, there are many different habitats.

Gardens and parks
Gardens, parks, allotments and community gardens can all be great habitats for wildlife.

Buildings
Many types of wildlife live right alongside humans. Mice, flies, spiders and birds often live in or around our homes.

Rivers, ponds and canals
Wherever there is water, there is also lots of wildlife!

Other urban spaces
Towns and cities are full of surprising places to find plants and animals. Look for them in cemeteries, school fields, overgrown areas and road and railway verges.

WHAT TO LOOK OUT FOR

To identify wildlife, you need to put together the clues that tell you what something is. To start with, it helps to know about the different wildlife groups. Here are some animal groups ...

Birds

Birds are animals with feathers and beaks. They have two legs and two wings. Most of them can fly. They lay eggs.

Birds have very light, honeycomb-like bones. This helps with flying.

Mammals

Most mammals have fur or hair, as well as four legs and a tail. In most of the mammals you will see, such as foxes, squirrels and rabbits, it's quite clear that they have four legs. But with bats the front legs are wings, and with seals the legs are flippers. Mammals feed their young on milk made by the mother.

Humans belong to this group of animals.

Amphibians

Amphibians are animals that are able to live both on land and in water. Most amphibians lay eggs that hatch into tadpoles, which live in water and breathe through gills. Most amphibians have smooth, damp skin, but some, like toads, have leathery and bumpy bodies.

smooth skin

Spring and summer are the best times to see amphibians. Look for them in or near ponds. Frogs and toads may hide under logs or stones in your garden.

four legs

Reptiles

Reptiles are animals with scaly skin. Altogether there are six species of reptiles in the UK: three snakes and three lizards.

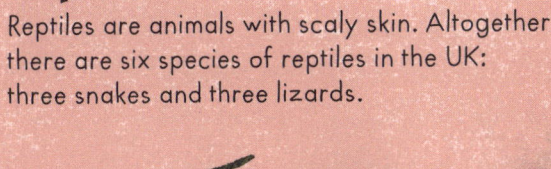

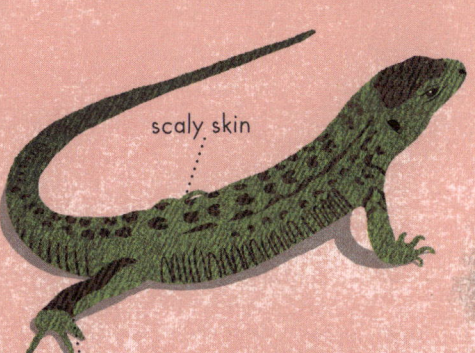

scaly skin

scaly skin

four legs

Reptiles hibernate in winter and come out in summer. They need to warm up in the sun to get enough energy to move around.

no legs

Fish

Fish are animals that live in water. They breathe through gills. Instead of legs they have fins, and they have streamlined bodies so that they can swim well. They have scaly skin.

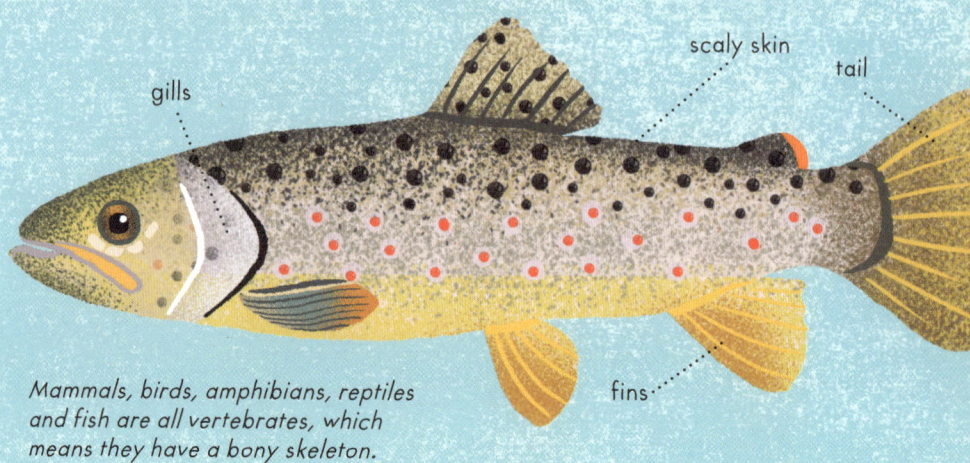

Mammals, birds, amphibians, reptiles and fish are all vertebrates, which means they have a bony skeleton.

Insects

Insects are one of the biggest and most varied groups of animals on the planet. Ants, ladybirds, bees, grasshoppers, flies and butterflies are all insects. They do have a few things in common, though. Their bodies are made up of three distinct parts: the head, thorax and abdomen. They all have six legs. Most of them have wings. They have amazing life cycles, with young that look completely different from the adults.

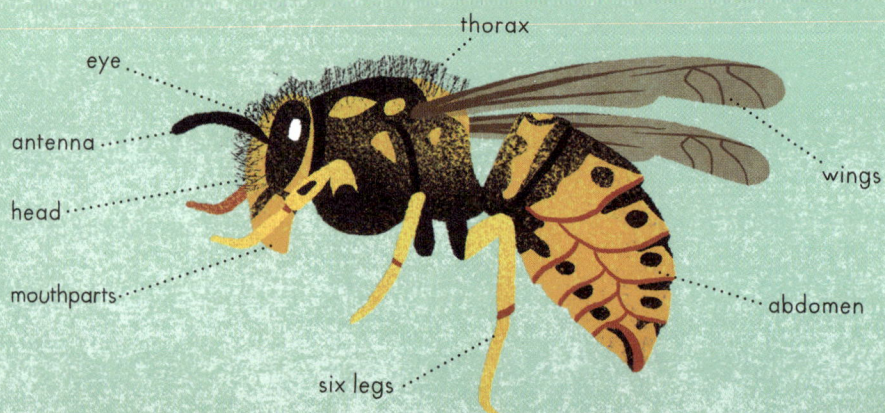

Spiders

Spiders' bodies are made up of two distinct parts: the head and thorax joined together, and the abdomen. They have eight legs and no wings. They have venomous fangs, many eyes and make silk in their bodies – some of them use this silk to spin elaborate webs.

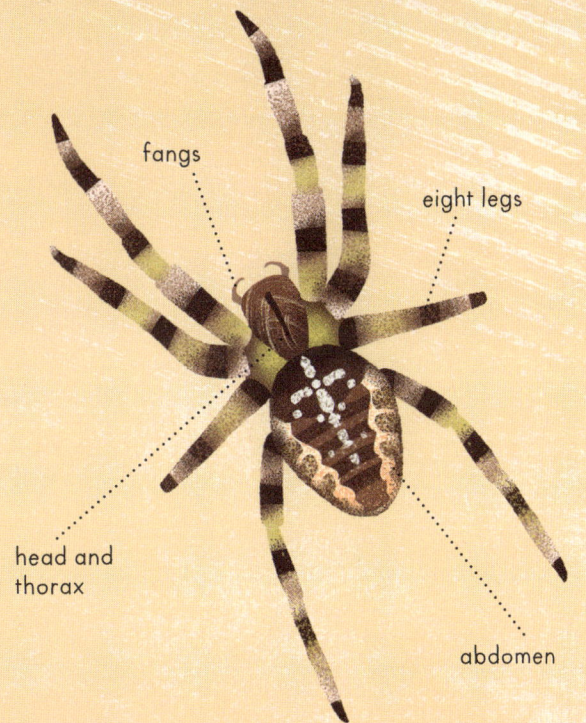

fangs

eight legs

head and thorax

abdomen

Other invertebrates

Invertebrates are animals without a backbone, sometimes called minibeasts. They have soft bodies – some kinds are protected by armour or shells but some aren't. Insects and spiders are two groups of invertebrates, but there are many, many more. Here are just a few:

Crustaceans, like woodlice, have jointed legs and a hard shell that protects them.

Snails have a soft body protected by a hard shell. Their cousins include slugs, which don't have a shell at all.

Earthworms have a soft body made up of lots of segments, and no legs.

Plants

Plants have green leaves. They make their own nutrients using their leaves and sunlight instead of eating food like animals do. They grow in one place rather than moving around. Many of them have flowers and make seeds.

Trees
Trees have a thick, stiff woody stem called a trunk, as well as woody branches and twigs.

Flowers
Many plants are known mostly for their flowers — from little daisies to tall plants such as rosebay willowherb.

Other plants
Some plants don't flower at all, for example ferns and mosses.

Fungi
Fungi aren't animals or plants. They belong to a different group altogether. The main fungus lives hidden in the soil. The part you see is called the fruit. Many are poisonous, so don't touch them.

How to use this book

The main section of this book is a nature guide. It will help you to name many of the animals, plants and fungi that you might see in towns and cities across the UK and Ireland.

Fact box

For many of the animals and plants in the nature guide you will find handy information in a fact box. Here is the key:

- ✏️ tells you the height — for animals this is measured from its head to its tail, and it is the height of an adult. For plants this is the average tallest height when it is fully grown
- 📅 tells you if it only grows, appears or visits at a certain time of year
- 🏠 tells you where the animal lives or where the plant grows (its habitat)
- 🔊 describes the animal's call or song
- 🌿 tells you what the animal eats

Descriptions

The descriptions tell you what each animal or plant looks like and give information about its behaviour or where you might find it.

Pictures

The pictures show what each animal or plant looks like — its shape, colour and patterns. They may show you how an animal sits, stands or perches or how a plant grows. They show you if the male and female look different from each other, and sometimes if the young look very different too.

BIRDS
House sparrow

The house sparrow is a very well-known bird of towns and cities. The male has a grey cap, black bib and brown-and-black feathers on its back. The female is plainer. House sparrows are happy living near people. They often make their nests in holes in buildings, in nestboxes and in garden bushes and hedges. Listen out for their noisy chirps.

house sparrow
- 14–15 cm
- towns and cities, gardens, parks, farmland
- chirps and chirrups
- seeds, scraps, greenflies, caterpillars

house sparrow (female)

house sparrow (male)

House sparrows are very sociable and sometimes nest in groups of 10 to 20 birds.

Robin

The robin is a little brown bird with a bright orange-red breast. Look out for it in gardens and parks, bobbing its head up and down and searching for worms, seeds and fruit. Robins are bold around humans, so they are one of our most familiar garden birds. They sing all year round to keep other robins away from their territory.

In cities, where it is very noisy in the daytime, robins sometimes even sing at night.

robin

robin
- 12–14 cm
- almost every habitat
- *tic tic* call, sweet song all year round
- spiders, beetles, flies, worms, berries, grain

Wren

The wren is a tiny brown bird with a pale stripe above its eye, and a tail that sticks up. It lives anywhere there are insects to eat and little cracks or gaps to nest in. Wrens can be hard to spot because they are so small, but listen for a loud, rattling song and wait for one to dart out of its hiding place.

wren
- 9–10 cm
- almost every habitat
- sharp *tik tik* call, loud, rattling song
- insects, other invertebrates

wren

During its nesting season, the male wren builds several nests. The female chooses the best one to lay her eggs in.

BIRDS

Great tit
The great tit has a black head, white cheeks, green back and a yellow breast with a black stripe down the middle. It is the largest member of the tit family. Great tits get on well in towns and cities. They also shoo away other birds to make sure they get the best food at feeding stations. Their loud call sounds like a squeaky gate.

Chaffinch
The chaffinch is a small, brightly coloured bird. The male is rusty-red with a blue-grey cap and chestnut back with a green patch, while the female is pale brown with flashes of pale green and yellow. Both genders have black-and-white wings. You'll usually hear chaffinches before you see them, thanks to their loud song and range of calls.

chaffinch (male)

chaffinch (female)

Goldfinch

The goldfinch is a small, colourful finch with a red, white and black face and a yellow band on its wings. Once only birds of the countryside, their numbers are booming in town and city suburbs, where they are regular visitors to feeders. Look for their dancing flight and listen for their tinkling calls.

Long-tailed tit

This tiny acrobatic bird lives up to its name, as its tail is twice as long as its body! The long-tailed tit has a black and pink back, a black-and-white striped head and is pale pink underneath. They are highly social and live in large family groups. In winter, they even form flocks with other tits and forage for food with them in parks and gardens.

Blue tit

The blue tit is one of our best-known garden birds. It has a yellow breast, white cheeks and a bright blue cap. In winter, blue tits are some of the liveliest, noisiest visitors to garden bird feeders and sometimes chase the other birds away. In spring they will happily use nest boxes, where they can lay up to 14 eggs.

BIRDS

Blackbird

The adult male blackbird is black with a bright orange beak and yellow rings around its eyes. The female is brown and the young are brown and spotty. Blackbirds are common in towns and cities and especially like living in gardens. The blackbird's loud, mellow, musical song is often voted one of the most beautiful of Britain's birdsongs.

blackbird
- 24–25 cm
- woodland, parks, gardens
- shrill *chink chink chink* call and rich song
- insects, worms, berries

blackbird (female)

blackbird (male)

When the male and female bird look different, this is known as sexual dimorphism.

Swift

The swift is dark brown-black with long, curved wings and a short, forked tail. Swifts fly high and are some of the fastest fliers in the bird world. In summer, you'll hear them screaming as they race past high in the sky. Swifts nest in buildings, so towns and cities are good places for them.

swift

UK swifts are declining in numbers, but special swift nestboxes can help give them safe places to live.

swift
- 16–17 cm
- summer
- towns, lakes
- harsh, screaming screech
- flying insects

Pied wagtail

The pied wagtail is a small black, white and grey bird. The male has a black back and the female's is grey. Pied wagtails can be seen in car parks, town centres, roofs, lawns, playing fields and gardens. Look for one wagging its tail up and down or chasing insects.

pied wagtail (female)

pied wagtail (male)

On winter nights, pied wagtails roost huddled up in big groups. They sometimes do this right in the town centre, among the hustle and bustle.

pied wagtail
- 18 cm
- countryside and towns
- sharp *chizik* flight call, twittering song
- flies, caterpillars, other insects

BIRDS
Feral pigeon

Also called the town pigeon, the feral pigeon is usually grey, although it can also be black, white or brown. It often has a green and purple shiny patch on its neck and black wing bars. Feral pigeons are found almost everywhere, but are common in towns and cities, where there is plenty of food and where buildings mimic their natural cliffside nesting sites.

feral pigeon

feral pigeon
- 31–35 cm
- almost every habitat
- cooing calls
- grain and other seeds, scraps of humans' food

Woodpigeon

The woodpigeon is grey with green and white patches on its neck and a pinkish-mauve breast. It is our largest and most common pigeon and it is just as common in towns as in the countryside. Look out for white bars on its wings when it flies.

Pigeons and doves feed their chicks a special 'milk' they make in their throats.

woodpigeon

woodpigeon
- 40–43 cm
- almost every habitat
- five-part call *coo-COO-coo, coo-coo*
- grain, plant buds, leaves and seeds, especially cabbage and peas, beetles and other insects

Collared dove

The collared dove is smaller than a woodpigeon. It is pinkish-grey with a black 'collar' on its neck and deep red eyes. These doves are usually found in pairs, but flocks can form in places with plenty of food.

collared dove

collared dove
- 32 cm
- farmland, parks, gardens
- three-part call *coo-COO-coo*
- seeds, grains, buds, shoots

ring-necked parakeet (female)

ring-necked parakeet
- 38 – 42 cm
- woodland, parks, gardens
- sharp, screeching call
- fruits, berries, nuts, seeds

ring-necked parakeet (male)

Ring-necked parakeet

The ring-necked parakeet has bright green plumage and a red bill. The male has a black and rosy-pink ring around its neck, while the female's is light green. These parrots were brought to the UK from Asia and Africa as exotic pets. Over the years, many escaped and large feral populations are now found in cities across the UK, especially in large gardens and parks.

BIRDS

Carrion crow

The carrion crow is a large, all-black crow with a thick black beak and a glossy sheen. Its name comes from its diet of carrion (dead animals), but it's a resourceful bird and will pretty much eat anything. It is mostly solitary, but crows from neighbouring territories often work together to chase off intruders.

carrion crow

carrion crow

- 45–47 cm
- farmland, woods, parks, gardens, towns and cities
- deep, cawing *kraaa kraaa*
- carrion, young birds and mammals, eggs, insects, worms, grain, seeds, fruit, shellfish

Jackdaw

The jackdaw is a black crow with a silvery patch on the back of its neck and pale eyes. It is our smallest member of the crow family. Jackdaws often nest in buildings, and you might see them perched on chimneys and rooftops, or walking along pavements looking for food.

jackdaw

- 33–34 cm
- farmland, woods, towns
- sharp *jack jack* and higher-pitched *kyow*
- insects, grain, seeds, fruit, berries, eggs, young birds, rubbish

jackdaw

In captivity, magpies have been known to imitate human speech.

Magpie

The magpie is a black and white crow, though its wings and tail are iridescent and can look purplish blue or green in the light. Magpies are noisy and chatter with each other as they fly. They are famous for collecting all sorts of objects to decorate their nests.

magpie
- 44–46 cm
- woods, farmland, towns, gardens, parks
- loud rattling sound
- fruit, berries, insects, worms, other birds' eggs and young, carrion (dead animals)

magpie

Starling

The starling looks black but in fact its feathers are shiny purple and green, with lots of white spots in winter. Starlings make a great variety of calls, tweets, chirps and clicks and are brilliant mimics. They can copy other birds' calls and even ringtones and car alarms.

starling
- 21.5 cm
- gardens, parks, farmland, towns and cities, rubbish tips, beaches
- complicated song with rattles and whistles, copies other birds' calls
- insects and their larvae, worms, spiders, berries, fruit

starling

On winter evenings, starlings gather in huge flocks called murmurations. Brighton, Blackpool and Aberystwyth are well-known places to see them.

BIRDS
Mute swan

The mute swan is a large, graceful waterbird. It is white apart from its black legs, black feet and bright orange bill with a black bump on top. It has a long neck that it uses to reach deep into the water to feed on plants. Mute swans are a common sight on ponds, rivers and canals and are generally happy to live around humans. When they are little, the cygnets (young) ride on their parents' backs to keep warm and stay safe from predators such as pike.

Mute swans usually pair for life.

mute swan

cygnets (young)

mute swan
- 125–155 cm
- lakes, rivers, canals
- loud hiss when angry
- water plants, insects, snails

Watch out – mute swans will hiss if you get too close!

Canada goose

The Canada goose is a large waterbird. It has a long black neck, white cheeks and chin and a greyish-brown body. You can see flocks in parks — they swim in ponds and lakes and waddle about on grass nearby. Brought here from their native North America, they now live as wild birds throughout the UK.

Canada goose
- 56–110 cm
- lakes, rivers, canals
- loud trumpeting
- roots, grass, leaves, seeds

Canada goose

Egyptian goose

The Egyptian goose is a sandy brown and grey goose with dark eye patches as well as flashes of white and shiny green under each wing. Originally from Africa, Egyptian geese in the UK mainly live in parks but can sometimes be found in farmland and grassland elsewhere in southern England.

Egyptian goose
- 63–73 cm
- parks, farmland, wetlands, grassland
- coarse honking call
- grass, seeds

Egyptian goose

BIRDS

Mallard

The mallard is the commonest duck in the world. It's also the most well-known and the one you are most likely to see in towns and cities. The male has a dark green head and yellow beak, and a bright flash of shiny blue on its wing that really stands out when it flies. The female is speckled brown and she has the shiny blue flash too. Watch as a mallard tips itself upside down to reach for food.

mallard (male)

mallard (female)

mallard
- 50 – 65 cm
- ponds, lakes, rivers, canals, marshes
- quiet, rasping call (male); *quack, quack* (female)
- seeds, plants, insects, shellfish, small fish

duckling (young)

Mandarin duck

The male mandarin duck has an array of colourful feathers, including two orange ones that stick up like sails on its back. The female is mainly brown and grey with a pale eye stripe. These pretty but shy birds were introduced from Asia and first escaped from parks into the wild in the 1930s.

mandarin duck
- 41–49 cm
- parks, wetlands, woodlands
- whistle (male); squeaky *quack* (female)
- insects, water plants, seeds

mandarin duck (female)

mandarin duck (male)

Tufted duck

The tufted duck is easy to spot by the tuft or crest on the back of its head. Males are black and white, females are dark brown and both have yellow eyes. Watch them dive time and time again to catch food. These ducks gather in large flocks in winter.

tufted duck
- 40–47 cm
- lakes, parks
- mostly silent
- shellfish, insects, water plants

tufted duck (female)

tufted duck (male)

BIRDS

Grey heron

The grey heron is a very large bird with long legs, a long neck and a sharp, dagger-like beak. It has a grey back and a white head with a black stripe. An expert at catching fish, the grey heron stands very still, watching fish in the water, then quickly skewers its prey and swallows it whole.

grey heron
- 90–98 cm
- lakes, rivers, marshes, estuaries
- deep croak
- mainly fish, also frogs and small mammals

grey heron

kingfisher

When grooming, grey herons use their toe like a comb to brush their feathers.

kingfisher
- 16–17 cm
- slow-flowing rivers, lakes, canals
- sharp, high-pitched *zeee*
- small fish, water insects

Kingfisher

The kingfisher is a small bird with a shiny turquoise back and wings, an orange belly and a long, strong beak. It is shy and moves fast, so despite its bright colours it is hard to see. Kingfishers are becoming more common in some towns and cities, a sign that the water quality in their rivers and canals is improving.

Coot

The coot is a waterbird. It is black except for its white beak, forehead and pale legs and feet. Its toes have lobed flaps of skin, which act in the same way as webbed feet when swimming. Coots are very quarrelsome birds and often fight each other.

coot
- 36–38 cm
- lakes, ponds
- loud *kowk*
- algae, water plants, shellfish, snails, insects

coot

moorhen
- 32–35 cm
- lakes, ponds, ditches, rivers
- loud *kruuuk*
- water plants, berries, worms, snails, spiders, insects, small fish, eggs

Moorhen

The moorhen is a bird that is often mixed up with a coot, and the two are often seen in the same places. The moorhen is smaller, with a red and yellow beak, white on its side and under its tail, and long, green legs and toes. Watch moorhens bob their heads back and forth as they swim.

moorhen

Young moorhens help raise their baby brothers and sisters.

chick (young)

BIRDS

Herring gull

The herring gull is a large bird. The adult is white, with a grey back and wings and a yellow beak with a red spot. While it is young, it has mottled brown feathers and a dark beak. Look out for its pink legs, which help tell it apart from other gulls. Herring gulls cope well in towns and cities and often nest on roofs. They eat everything from fish and bird eggs to scraps of people's food.

herring gull (young)

herring gull

herring gull

- 55–67 cm
- seaside, rivers, towns and cities
- various loud mewing and wailing cries
- carrion, seeds, fruit, insects, fish, eggs, young birds, small mammals, scraps of humans' food

Black-headed gull

The black-headed gull is a smallish gull. Its name is a bit misleading because its head is chocolate-brown. In winter, it turns white with just a small brown spot. You'll see these gulls at the coast, in farmland, in playing fields and in parks. They are sociable and noisy and gather in large flocks.

black-headed gull
- 34–37 cm
- coasts, rivers, fields, rubbish tips
- harsh *keeyar* call
- worms, insects, spiders, slugs, crabs, small fish, carrion, scraps of humans' food

black-headed gull

BIRDS

Peregrines are specialist pigeon hunters, and there are plenty of pigeons in towns and cities.

peregrine falcon

Peregrine falcon

The peregrine falcon is a medium-sized bird of prey. Look for its black head and 'moustache' and white cheeks. Peregrine falcons are brilliant hunters and hold the record for being the fastest animals in the world. Many cities have peregrines living in them. They nest in tall, inaccessible places that are the equivalent of rocky cliffs: on cathedral towers, bridges, the tops of office blocks and power stations.

peregrine falcon

- 39–57 cm
- hilly areas, towns and cities
- harsh, cackling *kek-rek-rek* when nesting
- birds

Kestrel

The kestrel is a bird of prey with a fanned tail and pointed wings. You may see one hovering by the roadside. It looks completely still except for its quivering wings, then it will dive fast to catch its prey. Like all birds of prey, kestrels have excellent eyesight.

Female birds of prey are typically larger and heavier than the males.

kestrel (female)

sparrowhawk
- 28 – 41 cm
- forests, farmland, towns and cities
- chattering *kew-kew-kew* when nesting
- small birds

kestrel
- 30 – 36 cm
- open areas with rough grassland, towns and cities
- shrill *ki-ki-ki-ki-ki*
- voles, other small mammals, small birds, large insects

Sparrowhawk

The sparrowhawk is a small bird of prey. The male has a grey back and a rusty-red chest, while the female has a brown back and distinctive white 'eyebrows', giving it a fierce expression. Both have a barred pattern on their front. Sparrowhawks fly very fast. They chase and snatch small birds in flight and even from feeders.

sparrowhawk (male)

MAMMALS

Leftover food scraps make up about half of an urban fox's diet. Most animals would get sick on such a diet, but luckily urban foxes have strong stomachs and immune systems.

fox

- 105 cm, including 40 cm tail
- countryside, towns and cities
- barking yelp, various shrieks
- birds, bird eggs, small mammals (especially rodents), insects, worms, leftover human food

fox

Fox

The fox has red-brown fur and a long bushy tail, sometimes with a white tip. It has sharp hearing, a good sense of smell and large, sharp canine teeth for seizing and piercing its prey. It will eat almost anything, from worms to mice, rabbits and leftover human food. Foxes usually come out at night, but in towns and cities they are bold and you may see them in the daytime.

A male fox is called a dog and a female is called a vixen.

Though they mostly scavenge, urban foxes will hunt rats and mice. This helps keep pest numbers down in urban areas.

Young cubs have blue eyes but adults' eyes are amber-coloured.

MAMMALS

House mouse

If you see a mouse in your home or around buildings, it is probably a house mouse. It has grey-brown fur, big eyes, a pointy face and a long scaly tail. House mice are agile and acrobatic. They are very capable climbers, jumpers and swimmers, and their flexible skeletons allow them to squeeze into very tiny spaces, even those as small as the width of a pencil.

house mouse

- 7–10 cm plus tail 13–20 cm
- farmland, warehouses, sheds, garages, houses, rubbish tips
- squeaks
- almost anything

Despite what you see in cartoons, this animal's favourite food isn't actually cheese. It prefers grains, seeds, fruit and insects.

house mouse

Red squirrel

The red squirrel has russet fur, tufty ears and a bushy tail. It is our native squirrel, but it is now a rare sight in the UK because grey squirrels, introduced from North America in the 19th century, pushed the reds out. It is only found in a few places in the UK, but in those areas it can live in towns and cities as well as in its usual forest habitats.

Grey squirrel

The grey squirrel is larger than the red squirrel, with a long, bushy tail. It is very common and easy to spot. Look out for grey squirrels scampering across the ground and up and down trees in town parks and gardens or boldly approaching humans.

grey squirrel
- 24–28.5 cm plus tail 19–24 cm
- woods, parks, gardens
- chattering noise to chase off intruders
- nuts, acorns, seeds, fungi, tree bark, leaves, shoots, buds, flowers

grey squirrel

MAMMALS

More and more otters are being spotted in urban waterways, which suggests the pollution levels in the water are dropping and those rivers are becoming healthier.

otter
- up to 130 cm
- rivers, lakes, seaside, canals
- high-pitched squeak
- fish

otter

In the 1970s, otters nearly went extinct in the UK because of river pollution and hunting, but they are gradually coming back now.

Otter

The otter is a sleek, strong, swimming predator with a flat head, long brown body, long tail and webbed feet. It has thick, oily fur that is warm and waterproof. It can swim under water for up to 400 metres and dive for up to a minute to catch its prey, mostly small fish. Otters are happy in freshwater or seawater.

Water vole

The water vole is a plump, brown vole with a chubby face, small ears and a hairy tail. It lives along rivers, streams and canals and around ponds. Water vole numbers overall have fallen, but they have recently started living in some cities. There are projects to help protect them in Glasgow, York and London, for example.

Brown rat

The brown rat has large ears, a pointy face, long whiskers and a scaly tail. Brown rats are omnivorous, and so eat more or less anything. They are particularly common in towns and cities, where there's lots of human food waste for them to eat, and live in burrows, under buildings and even in sewers.

brown rat
- 15–27 cm plus tail 25–51 cm
- almost everywhere
- squeaks, chirps, hissing
- almost anything

brown rat

MAMMALS

Red deer

The red deer is a large animal with a majestic, rich red-brown coat. Males, called stags, have long, branched antlers while the females, called hinds, are smaller and do not grow antlers. In the autumn, stags bellow to show how strong they are, and fight using their antlers as weapons. Though mountains and open moors are its natural habitat, the red deer can be found in many large parks across the UK.

red deer (female)

Antlers are bony growths that develop, drop off and regrow every year. When new, they are covered with a soft furry skin called velvet, but the deer soon rubs this off.

red deer (male)

red deer
- up to 230 cm
- woods, moors, mountains, large parks
- loud, bellowing calls
- grass, heather, lichens

Roe deer

The roe deer is a deer with a red-brown coat and a white chin. It has a black nose, large furry ears and a white patch on its rear. You might see them in parks, gardens or even wandering down the street.

Male roe deer are called bucks and females are does.

roe deer
- 90–130 cm
- woods, fields, farmland, gardens
- barking sound when alarmed
- tree shoots, leaves, bushes, brambles

roe deer (male)

roe deer (female)

Muntjac deer

The muntjac is a small deer. Males have short antlers and long canine teeth that stick out of their mouth. The deer are native to Asia and were brought to a park in Bedfordshire around 1900. They escaped and have since spread throughout the UK.

muntjac deer
- 45–52 cm
- woods, wetlands, towns, gardens
- loud barking sound
- shrubs, trees, grass, plants, fungi

Muntjacs can damage habitats by eating new shoots and young plants, preventing new trees from growing.

muntjac deer (male)

MAMMALS

Rabbit

The rabbit has long ears, long legs and a bouncing, hopping gait. It has grey-brown fur and big eyes on the sides of its head. Always on the lookout for danger, if it spots a predator, it will thump on the ground to warn others and dash into its burrow. In urban areas, it can be found in parks, gardens and cemeteries.

rabbit
- 40 cm
- woods, farmland, sand dunes, roadsides, large gardens
- usually silent but squeals when distressed
- grass, crops, green leaves

rabbit

A rabbit eats its own poo! Its gut cannot properly digest grass the first time round.

Mole

The mole is a small mammal with soft black fur, tiny eyes and a pink snout. It has big front paws with strong claws and it uses them like shovels to dig out tunnels. It has poor eyesight and finds its way underground by touch.

mole
- 12 cm
- farmland, grassland, woods, parks, gardens
- loud squeak
- worms, slugs, bug larvae

mole

It's rare that you will see a mole, but you will see the results of their digging – piles of soil called molehills.

Badgers track worms with their amazing sense of smell, which is 800 times more sensitive than a human's.

Badger

The badger has grey fur and is well-known for its black-and-white striped, pointed face. It has a stocky body, with strong legs and big claws for digging. Badger families live underground in homes called setts, which have a network of tunnels and sleeping rooms. Though not as common in urban areas as foxes, badgers can live in towns and cities as long as there's enough cover for them to build their setts, and parks and gardens where they can find earthworms to eat.

badger
- 90 cm
- woods, parks, gardens
- various calls, including growls, grunts, purrs, barks and squeaks
- worms, insects, seeds, fruit, birds' eggs, carrion (dead animals)

badger

MAMMALS

Common pipistrelle

Bats are the only true flying mammals. They come out at night and navigate in the dark by making very high-pitched sounds and listening out for echoes. This is called echolocation. The common pipistrelle is the bat you are most likely to see. Look out for it on summer evenings just as it gets dark.

These bats are excellent hunters and may catch as many as 3,000 flies and midges every night.

common pipistrelle

common pipistrelle
- 3.5–4.5 cm (wingspan 20 cm)
- April–October
- farmland, woods, towns, gardens, moorland
- very high-pitched squeaks and clicks
- midges, other small insects

brown long-eared bat
- 3.7–5.2 cm (wingspan 20–30 cm)
- April–October
- woods, farmland, towns, gardens
- very quiet squeaks
- insects

Brown long-eared bat

As its name suggests, the brown long-eared bat has very big ears that are almost as long as its body. It flies very slowly, using both its eyes and ears to find food. It hovers above its prey and then seizes it.

brown long-eared bat

Hedgehog

The hedgehog is our only prickly mammal. It has a long snout and little black eyes, and its body is covered in spines. It uses these for defence, rolling up into a spiky ball if a predator comes near. Hedgehogs come out at night to hunt slugs, snails, worms and insects. Gardens are an important habitat for hedgehogs and they can roam up to 1.6 kilometres a night to find food.

hedgehog
- up to 30 cm
- April – October
- woods, farmland, parks, gardens, cemeteries
- noisy huffing and puffing sounds
- slugs, snails, worms, caterpillars, beetles

Hedgehog spines are a special variation of hair. They have between 5,000 and 7,000 of them.

hedgehog

In towns and cities, cemeteries are often wildlife havens. Plants and animals can thrive in these quiet, undisturbed green spaces.

AMPHIBIANS

Common frog

The common frog is one of our most familiar and best-loved pond animals. It has a green and brown body. Its long, strong back legs make it an expert at hopping, jumping and swimming. It catches insects, slugs and worms on its sticky tongue. As with all amphibians, a frog likes to stay damp, in wet grass or in ponds. Look out for two big eyes sticking out above the surface of a pond.

common frog
- up to 9 cm
- February – October
- garden ponds, lakes, wet moorlands
- mostly silent, but churring calls on spring evenings
- insects, slugs, worms

frogspawn (eggs)

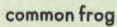
tadpole

froglet

Frogs and tadpoles

In spring, frogs arrive at a pond to mate and lay eggs. They lay clusters of eggs in jelly, called frogspawn. The eggs hatch into tiny creatures with tails, called tadpoles. Over many weeks the tadpoles get bigger and bigger. They grow legs and lose their tails, becoming froglets and then, finally, frogs.

Frogs have webbed feet.

Metamorphosis is when an animal changes shape as it grows from a baby into an adult.

common frog

Common toad

The common toad looks much like a frog, but has a larger, chunkier body and warty skin. It has strong back legs for swimming, and on land it usually walks instead of hopping. Toads are famous for their mass migrations back to their breeding ponds during spring, but in towns and urban areas, busy roads often block their migration paths. Volunteer groups gather at these spots to help the toads safely across the road.

common toad

 8–13 cm

 February – October

 grassland, moorland, ponds, rivers, lakes, farmland, woods

croak (male)

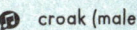 ants, beetles, worms, slugs

You can look up your local 'toad patrol' group online. Toads also need shelter to keep cool during the day – you can create one in your garden using just a flowerpot.

common toad

AMPHIBIANS

Smooth newt

Newts look a bit like lizards, with long bodies and long tails. Unlike lizards they swim in water and spend their time in damp places. The smooth newt is brownish-green with black stripes on its head and black spots along the body. In spring, the male grows an impressive crest along his back.

smooth newt
- 7–11 cm
- March–October
- ponds, rivers, woods, hedgerows, marshland
- tadpoles, crustaceans, molluscs (in water); insects, caterpillars, worms, slugs (on land)

smooth newt (male)

smooth newt (female)

Scientists think smooth newts use the common toad's mating calls to help them find ponds to breed in.

great crested newt
- up to 16 cm
- March–October
- ponds, woods, hedgerows, marshes
- tadpoles, crustaceans, molluscs (in water); insects, caterpillars, worms, slugs (on land)

Great crested newt

The great crested newt is a very big, dark-coloured newt. The male has a big, spiky crest on its back and looks like a miniature swimming dinosaur! Both sexes have white spots along their sides and orange, spotty bellies.

great crested newt (male)

Palmate newt

The palmate newt is smaller than the smooth newt, with a dark spotty back, a pale throat with no spots and a pale peachy underside. During the breeding season, the male has black webbing between his toes and a thin filament at the end of his tail. Like other newts, palmate newts visit ponds in springtime and spend the rest of the year in woodlands, hedgerows, marshes and grassland.

palmate newt

7–9 cm

March–October

ponds, rivers, heathland, hedgerows, marshland

frogspawn, tadpoles, crustaceans, molluscs (in water); insects, caterpillars, worms, slugs (on land)

palmate newt (female)

palmate newt (male)

Newts are protected by law and must not be disturbed.

REPTILES

Grass snake

The grass snake is the most common snake in Britain. It has a brown or olive-green back with black bars. You might see one swimming in a garden pond, looking for frogs, toads or tadpoles to eat. It is non-venomous and very shy – it might even play dead if cornered.

grass snake
- 90–150 cm
- April–October
- damp grass, ditches, pond banks, slow-moving streams
- hiss when caught
- frogs, small mammals, birds

grass snake

Unlike lizards, snakes do not have eyelids and so are unable to blink.

Adder

The adder is a snake with dry, scaly skin and a bold zigzag marking all the way down its back. It is our only venomous snake. Adders live in open woodland, but they've been seen in some city nature reserves. One example is Hounslow Heath, close to Heathrow Airport.

Adders do not eat every day – a large meal may last them a week or more.

adder
- up to 90 cm
- March–October
- heathland, grassland, sand dunes, woods, urban nature reserves
- hiss
- mainly mice and voles, also lizards, frogs, toads, small birds

adder (female)

Common lizard

The common lizard is widespread throughout the UK. It has thin stripes running down the side of its body and can be either pale brown, grey or pale green in colour. It stays very still, waiting for prey, then it runs very fast to catch insects to eat. Though it prefers wilder spaces, it is sometimes found in allotments and railway cuttings.

Lizards communicate through smell and body language, so they rarely make much noise.

slow-worm

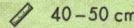 40 – 50 cm

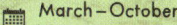 March – October

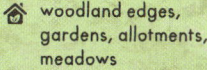 woodland edges, gardens, allotments, meadows

slugs, worms, snails, spiders

Slow-worm

The slow-worm looks like a worm or a snake, but it is actually a legless lizard. It is small with smooth, bronze-coloured skin. Males sometimes have blue spots, while females are bigger and have a dark stripe down their back. They shelter in mature gardens or in compost heaps, which are full of slugs and worms to eat.

If threatened, lizards can shed their tails to distract predators while they escape.

slow-worm (female)

FISH

pike

60–150 cm

lakes, slow-flowing rivers, canals

fish, frogs, crustaceans, invertebrates, small birds and mammals

Pike

The pike is a large fish with a long, torpedo-shaped body and a wide grin. It is a fearsome predator that lurks in vegetation and bursts out to ambush its prey of small fish and invertebrates. Though they typically prefer slow-moving rivers and lakes with lots of plant life, pike can be found in urban canals, particularly in areas where bridges and moored boats can provide them with cover.

A large female pike can lay up to 500,000 eggs.

pike

Pike are unfussy eaters and will hunt and eat whatever they can, including ducklings, voles and even rats.

Common carp

The common carp is a large fish. It is grey-bronze with a rounded body and four barbels (like whiskers) on its top lip. It is a close relative of the goldfish, though it's much bigger. Carps were introduced to the UK in the medieval period for people to eat. They are often found in slow-moving bodies of water, where they feel around in mud to find food.

common carp
- 25 – 80 cm
- ponds, lakes, gravel pits, canals
- algae, seeds, insects, crustaceans, fish eggs

common carp

Perch

The perch is slightly greenish in colour with dark stripes like a tiger. It has a large spiny back fin. Its other fins and tail are red. Perch are common in most UK freshwater habitats, including urban canals.

perch
- up to 25 cm
- large ponds, lakes, reservoirs, canals, rivers
- crustaceans, fish, invertebrates

perch

FISH

Chub
The chub is greenish silver with round, reddish fins and a dark tail. Shoals of chub often swim near the surface of rivers and streams, which make them quite easy to spot.

Bream
The bream is a medium-sized fish and is dark brown-bronze in colour. It is related to the carp and has a similar shape. It lives in large ponds, lakes and slow-moving rivers and canals.

Brown trout
The brown trout is a golden-coloured fish speckled with dark, reddish spots. It lives in fast-flowing rivers and is a keen hunter. Its diet consists of insects, crustaceans and small fish, but a large trout might also eat swimming voles and mice.

Three-spined stickleback
The three-spined stickleback has a small brown body with a silvery side and three spines sticking out of its back. It is the most common freshwater fish in UK canals and rivers, and is particularly fond of shallow, weedy water.

Gudgeon
The gudgeon is a small, thin fish. It is dark in colour with a dark line along its side. It has two barbels (like whiskers) near its mouth, which it uses to feel for prey on the riverbed.

European eel
The European eel looks like a snake, but it is actually a long, narrow fish. It is famous for its long migration from freshwater rivers in Europe all the way across the Atlantic Ocean. Once common in London rivers, it is now critically endangered and conservation efforts are being made to boost its numbers.

MINIBEASTS

Garden snail

The garden snail is found wherever there are plenty of plants for it to eat. Like all snails, it has a hard shell, which it uses both as a shelter and to protect its soft, slimy body. It moves along slowly on a long muscle called a foot that stretches the whole length of its body. Snails leave behind a trail of mucus as they go, making surfaces slippery so they can easily glide along.

garden snail
- 4 cm across (shell)
- gardens, farmland, hedgerows
- plants, algae

garden snail

Earthworm

The earthworm is a pink-grey worm that lives in soil. Its soft body is made up of lots of segments. Earthworms play an important role in nature — by eating dead plant matter and creating air pockets in the earth as they burrow, they create healthy soils so new plants can grow.

earthworm
- up to 35 cm
- everywhere
- rotting plants and animals

earthworm

Earthworms breathe through their skin.

Garden slug

The garden slug looks like a snail without a shell. It also has one great long foot and moves along on a silvery trail of slime. Slugs come in all sorts of colours, such as brown, grey, black, yellow and orange (some even have leopard spots). They love eating garden plants and sometimes invade vegetable patches, making them unpopular with gardeners.

Slugs have a large hole just behind their head for breathing.

garden slug

Slugs have between 2,000 and 8,000 tiny teeth, which they use to rasp and scrape their food (a bit like a cheese grater).

garden slug

- up to 14 cm
- gardens, woodland
- plants, especially dead plants, carrion, dung

Every slug is male and female at the same time. Earthworms and most snails are too.

MINIBEASTS

Although strands of spider silk are very thin and easily broken, they are actually very strong. For their size, they are stronger than steel and tougher than Kevlar, the material used to make bulletproof vests.

> **garden spider**
> 9–15 mm
> May–November
> gardens, grassland, woods, farmland
> insects

garden spider

Spiders are very hairy and their hairs do different jobs. They use them for camouflage, hearing, gripping, smell and taste, and even as a hairbrush!

Garden spider

The garden spider is a large spider with a big round body and eight hairy legs. Its body is brown with white marks in the shape of a cross. Like all spiders, it has the amazing ability to spin silk. Every day, this spider builds a new spiral web as a sticky trap to catch insects. Then it kills the insects with a venomous bite before wrapping them in more silk to eat later.

Zebra spider

The zebra spider is a little spider covered in black-and-white stripes, just like a zebra. It is a jumping spider, and so rather than catching insects by spinning a web, it stalks and pounces on its prey.

Spiders have two large eyes in front and several smaller eyes. Look for the zebra spider's especially big black eyes.

Giant house spider

The giant house spider is a large spider with a dark hairy body and long legs. It is fast and can sprint up to half a metre per second. This common spider is shy and prefers quiet, undisturbed spaces to build its sheet-like webs, like behind furniture or in garages and attics.

Cellar spider

The cellar spider has a small pale body and long, very thin legs. It is almost always found indoors, where it thrives in the warm conditions and spins loose, messy webs high up in the corners of rooms.

MINIBEASTS

Black garden ant

The black garden ant is a tiny, busy insect. It has a black or dark brown body with a very thin 'waist', and strong, pincer-like jaws. It lives in a colony with around 15,000 other ants, who all have different jobs to do. There is a queen, who lays eggs, and thousands of workers or soldiers, who look after the nest, raise the larvae (young) and go out to find food.

black garden ant

black garden ant

- 3–5 mm
- March – October
- gardens, parks, farmland
- nectar, fruit, honeydew, seeds, other small insects

Common woodlouse

The common woodlouse is a grey creature with tough armoured plates along its back and seven pairs of little legs. It is a very unfussy eater and its diet includes leaf litter, rotting food, dead animals and even its own poo. Woodlice like to shelter in dark, damp spaces to avoid drying out.

common woodlouse

- 14 mm
- gardens, woods, farmland
- dead and decaying matter such as fallen leaves, rotting wood, fungi, fallen fruit, dead animals and dung

common woodlouse

Green lacewing

The green lacewing has a lime-green body and long antennae. It gets its name from the lacy patterns of veins on its large, see-through wings. In winter, it often hibernates in garden sheds.

green lacewing
- 10 – 15 mm
- April – October
- grassland, woods, towns, gardens
- aphids

Seven-spot ladybird

The seven-spot ladybird is one of our best-known insects. It is a kind of beetle, with hard wing cases like other beetles. It is bright red, with three black spots on each wing case and a seventh spot split between the two. It has black legs and a black-and-white head. Look out for ladybirds crawling up and down flower stems, gobbling up aphids.

green lacewing

seven-spot ladybird

Ladybirds are loved by gardeners because they eat damaging pests.

seven-spot ladybird
- 6 – 8 mm
- March – October
- gardens, grassland, woods, towns, cities, farmland
- aphids

MINIBEASTS

Housefly

The housefly has a hairy body with black and brown stripes, and large red compound eyes. It is one of the commonest insects in the world. The female lays batches of around 100 eggs at a time on rotting meat, dead animals or poo, the three primary food sources for the housefly, and these eggs hatch into larvae called maggots.

housefly

 7–9 mm

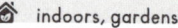 indoors, gardens

leftover human food, rotting meat, dung (adult and larva)

maggots (fly larvae)

Maggots feed on rotting meat and dead animals. This may sound disgusting but it is very useful as it helps clean up and recycle waste in the environment.

housefly

Cranefly
Also known as a daddy long-legs, the cranefly is a gangly insect with a thin body and very long legs. It is a clumsy flier and you might see one bumping into a lit window. When threatened, it sheds one of its long legs to provide a distraction while it escapes.

Bluebottle
The bluebottle is larger than the housefly. It has a shiny blue-black body with hairy bristles. Adult bluebottles only feed on nectar, and are particularly fond of plants with strong odours.

Marmalade hoverfly
The marmalade hoverfly is one of the UK's most common hoverfly species. It has a yellow and black stripy abdomen like a wasp. This is a disguise to trick predators into thinking it can sting. As the name suggests, hoverflies are expert fliers and can hover in mid-air, fly slowly or zoom backwards and forwards.

MINIBEASTS

Emperor dragonfly

The emperor dragonfly is Britain's largest dragonfly. The male has a long blue body, while the female is a duller greeny-blue. Both have huge green eyes and two sets of see-through wings. Like all dragonflies, it is an expert flier. It can reach speeds of over 30 kilometres per hour, can fly backwards, hover on the spot and even fly upside down.

emperor dragonfly (female)

emperor dragonfly (male)

nymph

Dragonfly and damselfly larvae are called nymphs. They live underwater and have gills for breathing. They grab and eat other water creatures, such as tadpoles.

emperor dragonfly

- 78 mm
- June – August
- large ponds, lakes, canals, rivers
- flying insects (adult); tadpoles, water insects, small fish (larva)

Common pond skater

The common pond skater is a grey insect with long legs, which it uses to skate over the surface of ponds, lakes and rivers. If another insect falls into the water, the common pond skater will glide over to it, pierce it with its sharp mouthparts and slurp out the insides.

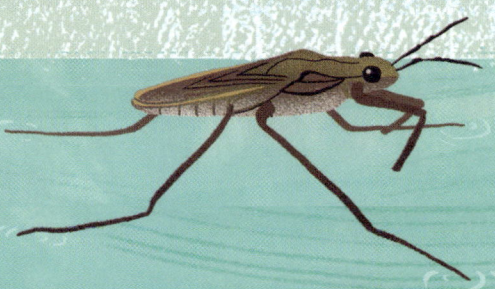

Whirligig beetle

The whirligig beetle is a tiny, glossy, blue-black beetle. It eats other insects that fall on the water's surface. Look out for groups of them whirling around in circles.

common backswimmer

Common backswimmer

The common backswimmer is a water bug with a brown, boat-shaped body and reddish eyes. It swims upside down and uses its oar-like back legs to row through the water. It finds and hunts small creatures by sensing the vibrations they make in the water.

common backswimmer

 14 mm

 ponds, lakes, canals

 insects, tadpoles, small fish

MINIBEASTS

Peacock
The peacock is a large, colourful butterfly. It is mostly red, with brilliant blue eyespots on each wing. These look like the markings on an Indian peacock's tail feathers and are there to confuse predators. You might spot a peacock butterfly sunning itself in your garden.

Peacock caterpillars are black with tiny white spots. They have lots of spikes along their bodies.

Small tortoiseshell
The small tortoiseshell is one of our best-known butterflies and one of our most colourful too. It boasts bright orange wings with black and yellow flashes and spots, as well as blue spots edged with black along all four wings. Its caterpillars love feeding on nettles.

eggs

caterpillar

chrysalis

A butterfly starts its life as an egg, which develops into a caterpillar. It then spends all its time eating and growing, and later develops a hard, protective shell called a chrysalis. Inside, it changes and eventually emerges as an adult butterfly.

Red admiral
The red admiral is a large red and black butterfly. It is found in almost every habitat and is a common visitor to gardens, where there is plenty of nectar for it to feed on (though it will also suck juices from rotting fruit).

orange-tip (male)

orange-tip (female)

Orange-tip
The male orange-tip butterfly has orange wingtips, while females are all-white with black wingtips and two black spots. Both sexes have a mossy grey-green pattern underneath their wings.

holly blue (male)

Holly blue
The holly blue is a small blue butterfly. It is pale blue above with dark tips to its front wings, and underneath, its wings are light and speckled with blue and black. It lays its puffy white eggs on ivy or holly.

MINIBEASTS

Brimstone moth
The brimstone moth has buttery yellow wings with chestnut brown blotches and silvery spots. Though it is a nocturnal moth, it tends to pick daytime resting places that are easily disturbed, such as bushes and low hanging branches, so might be seen flying during the day.

Cinnabar moth
The cinnabar moth is a small moth that flies day and night in grassy places. It is black and red with a pattern of lines and spots. Its caterpillars are striped black and orange and you may see groups of them feeding on ragwort plants.

cinnabar moth (caterpillars)

Jersey tiger moth
This black-and-cream striped moth has bright orange-red underwings with black spots. It uses its bright underwings to flash a warning to predators.

Elephant hawk-moth

The elephant hawk-moth is a large, colourful moth. It is mostly greenish brown and bright pink, and has white legs and antennae. At dusk, look out for this moth hovering around garden flowers that give off a stronger scent later in the day such as honeysuckle. Its caterpillars look like elephant trunks!

Large yellow underwing moth

The large yellow underwing moth has brown or grey front wings with a pattern like tree bark, and yellow-orange back wings. It rests during the day, but if it is disturbed, it will flash its boldly coloured underwings to surprise predators.

Peppered moth

This moth comes in two different kinds – one pale and one dark in colour. The pale kind lives in woodlands, where its colouring helps it disappear against light-coloured trees and lichen. The darker kind lives in urban areas, where it can blend in against walls and trees that have been darkened by pollution.

Garden tiger moth

The garden tiger moth is a colourful moth, with orange hindwings and big blue-black spots nestled underneath its chocolate brown and white forewings. These bright colours act as a warning sign to predators that the moth tastes bad so that they'll leave it alone.

MINIBEASTS

Red mason bee

The red mason bee is a small, gingery bee. It gets its name because the female is like a little mason, or builder. She lays her eggs in a tunnel in an old wall or piece of wood, puts a mixture of pollen and nectar in the tunnel for the larvae to eat when they hatch, then presses mud to seal up the tunnel entrance. Red mason bees are solitary bees.

red mason bee
- 6 – 11 mm
- March – June
- gardens, farmland, moorland, grassland
- nectar, pollen

red mason bee (female)

Some bees live in colonies with a queen and hundreds of workers. But solitary bees live alone. A female builds her own nest and lays her eggs there.

red-tailed bumblebee (male)

Red-tailed bumblebee
The red-tailed bumblebee is a mainly black bee with a red-orange bottom. The male has yellow markings on its abdomen and face. Watch out for this bee feeding on daisies, dandelions and thistles in the garden.

buff-tailed bumblebee

Buff-tailed bumblebee

The buff-tailed bumblebee is a big, hairy black-and-yellow bumblebee. The queen has a completely buff (pale brown) tail and workers have a white tail with a thin buff stripe. This bee buzzes around flowers, searching for nectar, and it prefers open, daisy-like flowers.

buff-tailed bumblebee
- 20–25 mm
- March–August
- gardens, towns, cities, grassland
- nectar

Common wasp

The common wasp is a flying, black-and-yellow stripy insect. Its bright colours act as a warning to other animals to keep away or risk being pricked by its venomous stinger. Though they are often disliked or feared, wasps are important pollinators and provide a garden pest-removal service by hunting insects to chew up and feed to their larvae.

wasp nest

common wasp
- 15 mm
- April–October
- most habitats
- nectar, fruit juices (adult); small insects and other invertebrates (larva)

common wasp

TREES

A single oak tree can provide habitat, food and shelter for thousands of other species.

oak
- 20–40 m
- woods, parks

Oak

The oak is a magnificent tree. It has a very thick trunk and a wide crown with many large branches. Its leaves have a very well-known shape, with wavy edges. In autumn, look out for its acorns (seeds that sit in little scaly cups on long stalks). An oak does not produce acorns until it is at least 40 years old, but can produce as many as 25 million in its lifetime.

TREES

silver birch

Silver birch bark has been used as paper for centuries.

Silver birch

The silver birch gets its name from its silvery-white bark, which is flaky and papery. It has thin, drooping branches with lots of small, heart-shaped leaves. In spring, the silver birch has flowers called catkins, sometimes known as 'lamb's tails'.

silver birch
- up to 30 m
- woods, towns and cities, gardens, moorland, grassland

Ash

The ash is a tall tree with pale grey bark and leaves made up of lots of long, slim leaflets. In autumn and winter, it has clusters of seeds, called keys, that hang in little bunches. It is a pretty tree, and so has been planted in abundance in parks, but since it can handle the higher levels of pollution, it also grows well in urban areas.

ash
- up to 15 – 35 m
- farmland, woods, towns and cities

ash

Sycamore

The sycamore is a large tree with leaves bigger than your hand. The leaves are tough and dark green and even look a bit like a hand, with five finger-like leaflets. Its seeds have wings that help them catch a breeze and float far away from the tree. The winged seeds are commonly known as 'helicopters'.

sycamore

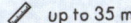
up to 35 m

parks, hedgerows, woods

Hawthorn
The hawthorn has sharp thorns and often grows in hedges. It has creamy-white blossom in spring, also known as May blossom. In autumn, it has red berries called haws, which birds love to eat.

Holly
The holly is known for its shiny, prickly leaves and bright red berries. The berries are poisonous to humans but many birds love to eat them. Holly is evergreen, meaning it keeps its leaves all year round.

TREES

London plane
- up to 35 m
- parks, gardens, along city streets

The London plane is the most common tree in Inner London. The total area of its leaves is more than that of any other tree in the city.

London plane

This tree is found in many other towns and cities in the UK — and in Paris and Dublin too.

London plane

The London plane is a tall tree with large leaves made of five triangular lobes. Its bark is scaly with a camouflage pattern. This species was cultivated by humans and doesn't grow wild, but is common in parks, gardens and streets in cities. In these places, it copes well with pollution and soil that has become hardened by traffic. It is very beneficial as an urban tree because it absorbs pollution and provides shade.

Horse chestnut

The horse chestnut is a giant tree, often found in parks, gardens and streets. It has large leaves made of five to seven big leaflets. In spring, it has flowers that stick up like white candles. In autumn, it has shiny seeds called conkers. They grow inside prickly cases.

Horse chestnuts are under attack from two diseases, so scientists are busy trying to find out how to help them.

horse chestnut

horse chestnut
up to 40 m
parks, gardens, roadsides

Beech

The beech is a tall tree with a wide crown. Its leaves are oval with slightly wavy edges. The new young leaves of a beech are very bright green. The green darkens throughout the summer and the leaves turn rich brown in autumn. The beech produces small, triangle-shaped nuts in spiny cases.

beech

beech
up to 40 m
woods, gardens

FLOWERS AND OTHER PLANTS

Daisy
The daisy is a small, cheerful-looking flower, with a centre like a yellow button surrounded by lots of thin, white petals (which are sometimes tinted with pink at the edges). It is one of the best-known wildflowers, and is found almost anywhere and at any time of year.

Daisies open in the daytime and close up at night.

White clover
White clover has flowers that look like white pom-poms. Its leaves have three lobes, and each lobe is heart-shaped with a pale band. The flowers produce lots of nectar, so bees and other pollinators love them.

Very rarely, a clover leaf has four lobes instead of three. Four-leaved clovers are thought to bring good luck.

Buttercup
The buttercup is a bright and glossy yellow flower. Each one has five round petals, and long, spindly green stems. Buttercups often grow in very large numbers, peppering entire lawns and gardens in sunshine-yellow.

Yellow corydalis
Yellow corydalis has small flowers like yellow trumpets. It often grows out of cracks in walls and pavements. It was first planted in the UK as a garden flower but has escaped into the wild. It provides early nectar for bees.

Forget-me-not
The forget-me-not is a small blue flower that grows in dry, sunny places such as hedges and woods, but also in cracks and crevices of roadways and walls. Each tiny flower has five blue petals with a yellow centre or 'eye'. It has grey-green, oblong, hairy leaves.

Dandelion
The dandelion has bright yellow flowers on tall, straight stems, and ragged leaves with pointy, tooth-shaped edges. Dandelions are often thought of as weeds, but they are very important — they provide nectar early in the year for more than 50 different insects, and their seeds provide food for birds.

Dandelion stems are hollow and ooze a milky juice if you break them.

Rosebay willowherb

The rosebay willowherb is a large plant with dark pink flowers. The flowers have four petals and lots of them grow together on tall, straight flower spikes. Its leaves are thin and pointed and it has light, fluffy seeds that blow on the breeze.

Herb robert

Herb robert has small pink flowers, reddish stems and feathery leaves. It grows in shady places, such as woods, hedges, rocks, walls and waste ground. Each little flower has five round petals and a pinky-red spike sticking out of the middle.

Bramble

The bramble is a prickly shrub that grows almost anywhere, covering the ground or scrambling up trees or walls. It has white or pale pink flowers followed by juicy blackberries. It is one of the most important plants for providing food and shelter for insects, spiders, birds and mammals, and it protects growing trees too.

Stinging nettle
The stinging nettle has pairs of hairy, heart-shaped leaves and hanging bunches of pale green flowers. The hairs on its leaves and stem can give a nasty sting, so humans tend to avoid it, though like the prickly bramble, it's a very important plant for insects.

Cow parsley
Cow parsley is a common plant with tall stems, feathery green leaves and lacy white flowerheads, which are made up of lots of tiny white flowers arranged in umbrella shapes. Many animals, from orange-tip butterflies to rabbits, like feeding on cow parsley plants.

There are species of toxic plants that are easily mistaken for cow parsley. To avoid any risk, never touch or pick this plant.

Common ragwort
Common ragwort has yellow starry flowers and feathery but tough leaves. It grows in meadows and on waste ground. It is one of the most important wildflowers in the UK because so many other creatures, especially butterflies and moths, depend on it. It is poisonous to horses and cattle, but these animals know to avoid eating it.

FLOWERS AND OTHER PLANTS

Ivy

Ivy is a woody evergreen climbing plant with dark green, glossy, oval or heart-shaped leaves. It grows up trees and walls as well as trailing along the ground. It has round domes of greenish flowers in autumn, and dark berries. It supports many insects and birds, which feed on it and nest among its dense leaves.

ivy

up to 30 m

towns, gardens, woods, coasts, farmland, rocky areas

ivy

Lichen

Lichens are fascinating living things. They are not plants, but each species of lichen is a partnership between a fungus and an alga. They can't survive on their own, only together, and are found on rocks and stones, branches and even on old leaves. There are about 1,800 species of lichen in the UK. Have a look for different shapes and colours.

Hart's tongue fern

The hart's tongue fern has bright green, tongue-shaped leaves. It mainly grows in damp, shady woodland, but can be found in towns and cities too. Look for it on walls and beside canals. Ferns do not have flowers, and instead of seeds they have spores.

Male-fern

The male-fern has lots of delicate, feathery-looking fronds. It grows in damp, shady places, such as woodlands, hedgerows and ditches. It was given its name because it is bigger than a very similar fern that is called the lady fern.

Moss

Mosses are tiny plants that grow in dense clumps in moist shady places. They can grow on a variety of surfaces, from trees, branches and rocks to walls, patios and pavements. They do not have any flowers or seeds and grow small, simple leaves. The UK has hundreds of different types of moss.

FUNGI

⚠ Fly agaric

The fly agaric is the toadstool we're used to seeing in fairy stories, cartoons and even video games. It is bright red with white spots and is umbrella-shaped with a thick white stem. Look for the white frill near the top of the stem. It grows in woodland, grassland and in parks, and often near birch or pine trees, especially if the trees are ancient. It is extremely poisonous.

Fungi shaped like umbrellas on stalks are also known as mushrooms and toadstools.

Shaggy inkcap

The shaggy inkcap is a tall toadstool with a white cap that is shaggy all over. Its cap is black underneath and sometimes drips inky black liquid.

Chicken of the woods

Chicken of the woods is a bright yellow frilly-looking fungus. It is a bracket fungus, which is a type of fungus that grows on tree trunks and looks like a shelf. This one mainly grows on oak tree trunks.

Common puffball

The common puffball looks just like its name suggests: a big white puffy ball. It grows in woodlands and by roadsides. When the puffball is mature, a hole grows in its centre. Spores puff out from this hole when something knocks the fungus.

Brown mottlegill

The brown mottlegill is a small mushroom with a brown cap and thin white stem. The cap is dark chestnut brown when wet and pale sandy brown when dry. It is also called the mower's mushroom because it often grows on lawns.

GET INVOLVED WITH WILDLIFE

In towns and cities

One way to get involved with nature is to help give it a place to live. Maybe your family has a garden, or there is one at your school or a community centre. Even the smallest green space can be a haven for wildlife and there is lots you can do to make it a good habitat.

Remember that animals need food, water, places to shelter and hide and somewhere to raise a family.

Go wild!
Wildlife doesn't like things to be too tidy! If you can find a corner where you can let wild nettles, ivy and brambles grow, you will entice all sorts of insects, birds and other animals into your garden.

Encourage adults to avoid using pesticides and other harmful chemicals, and use wildlife-friendly feed, fertiliser and pest control instead.

Home help
Give bugs and bees a helping hand by putting up bug or bee hotels for them to nest in. Or you can make your own home for solitary bees by putting some dry grass in a flowerpot and partly burying it in the ground.

Food and water

You can help birds by hanging bird feeders in trees or bushes. There are even feeders you can stick to a window. Any feeders need to be out in the open, and not near anywhere cats or other predators might hide.

Don't forget water — especially in summer when it is hard to find and in winter when it can freeze. A bird bath gives birds clean water to drink and somewhere to wash their feathers.

You can also help birds by growing plants that will appeal to the insects they feed on, or that have fruit or seeds they like to eat.

Creepy-crawly zone

Make a pile of dead logs in a hidden corner and you'll be creating a home for all sorts of crawling minibeasts. Rotting wood is food for earthworms, woodlice, millipedes, ants, slugs and some beetles. Then other beetles, spiders and earwigs as well as larger animals — such as toads, mice and birds — will come along and eat them!

More activities to try

Put up a nest box
You can buy a nest box from the RSPB or other good suppliers. With an adult's help, fix it at least two metres high on a tree or wall, facing somewhere between north and east to protect it from bad weather.

Nature walk
Why not try out your nature-spotting skills in a part of your town or city? It could be a park, or a built-up area, or a combination of the two. Don't forget to listen for bird calls and songs and other animal noises too.

Small safari
Go on the hunt for the smallest living things that are usually easy to overlook. Examine walls and tree trunks for different kinds of moss and lichen, look out for insects and spiders, have a close look at small wildflowers and seek out small leaves or seeds that have fallen from trees.

Flower food

You can make a little wildlife haven by growing plants that insects will love. You don't even need a garden for this — you can do it in pots by your door, on a balcony or even a window box.

Try planting:

crocus, lavender, scabious, marjoram, thyme, rosemary, verbena, violets, sunflowers, French marigold, foxglove, knapweed, meadow cranesbill

Another way to help pollinating insects is to let some weeds (many of which are wildflowers) grow.

Nature collage

Get inspired by urban nature and create a work of art! Paint or draw a picture, then add fallen leaves, twigs and seeds that you've found while you've been out exploring.

Join a club

There are lots of clubs you can join to share your love of wildlife with other people. You and your family can volunteer with the RSPB, or perhaps your school or local area has a nature or conservation club. You could even start your own!

Go on a field trip

Many towns and cities have nature reserves, where you can enjoy the great outdoors and meet all sorts of wildlife. Here are just a few you can visit around the UK and Ireland:

- Queen Elizabeth Olympic Park (London, England)
- Camley Street Nature Park (London, England)
- WWT London Wetland Centre (London, England)
- Chorlton Water Park (Manchester, England)
- Sefton Park (Liverpool, England)
- Sutton Park (Birmingham, England)

- RSPB Belfast Window on Wildlife (Belfast, Ireland)
- North Bull Island (Dublin, Ireland)

- RSPB Barons Haugh (Glasgow, Scotland)
- Bawsinch and Duddingston Wildlife Reserve (Edinburgh, Scotland)

- RSPB Conwy (Conwy, Wales)
- RSPB Newport Wetlands (Newport, Wales)

Some wildlife clubs and organisations

- *Buglife* www.buglife.org.uk
- *Butterfly Conservation* www.butterfly-conservation.org
- *The RSPB Wild Challenge* https://wildchallenge.rspb.org.uk
- *The National Trust* www.nationaltrust.org.uk
- *The Wildlife Trusts* www.wildlifetrusts.org/where_to_see_urban_wildlife

Record and share

Why not record your findings, perhaps in a notebook or by photographing or drawing what you see? You could make little videos of things you find. If you like, you can share your records. This is called citizen science and means you are helping scientists to find out more about animal and plant life. For example, you can take part in the RSPB Big Garden Birdwatch every January, Butterfly Conservation's Big Butterfly Count every July to August, The Woodland Trust's Nature's Calendar and many more.

Find out more

See what you can discover with these great books, webpages and free apps.

- *Bloomsbury RSPB Nature Guide: Birds; Minibeasts; Seashore* and *Wildlife*
- *RSPB Nature Tracker's Handbook* by Nick Baker (Bloomsbury, 2018) — a guide to nature tracks
- *Merlin Bird ID* by Cornell Lab — available from the app store
- *Seek* by iNaturalist — available from the app store
- *Tree ID* — British trees identification by the Woodland Trust — available from the app store
- *RSPB Live Wildlife Webcams* — www.youtube.com/RSPBvideo/streams

Glossary

abdomen the end section of an insect's body

antennae another word for feelers. Insects and some other invertebrates use their antennae for touching, smelling and tasting

bud leaf or flower before it has opened

canine teeth long pointed teeth that some mammals have

colony a very large number of the same type of creature all living together

conservation saving and looking after the environment and wildlife

cultivated when describing plants, it means a particular variety of plant has been raised and produced by humans rather than evolving naturally

dimorphism when members of the same species can come in two different physical forms based on certain traits, like age or sex

domestic tame or living with people. A domestic animal is a farm animal or a pet

dusk evening, when it is getting dark

echolocation finding the way or finding prey by making very high-pitched sounds and listening out for echoes

environment everything around us. It is made up of the air, ground, soil, and all living and non-living things

extinct died out altogether

eyespot a spot that looks like an eye

gills the parts of the body used for breathing in some underwater creatures

grooming when an animal brushes, combs or licks its body to keep clean

habitat the type of place where a particular animal or plant lives

hibernate go into a very deep sleep during the winter

hover fly almost on the spot, not moving forwards or backwards

larva insect young. Caterpillars, maggots and grubs are some other names for larvae

life cycle the different stages a living thing goes through in its life

lobe a rounded part of something such as the rounded section of a leaf

mate an animal's mate is the partner it has babies with. To mate means to come together to make babies

metamorphosis something changing into different forms as it goes through its life cycle. Tadpoles changing into frogs and caterpillars changing into butterflies are examples of metamorphosis

migration moving regularly or seasonally from one part of the world to another, usually to find a good feeding place or somewhere to breed

native an animal or plant that naturally lives or grows in a habitat and has not been brought from somewhere else

navigate work out where to go

nectar a sugary liquid made by flowers and eaten by many different animals

nutrients ingredients that animals and plants need to grow and stay healthy

nymph a dragonfly or damselfly larva

pollen a dusty substance made by flowers

pollinator an insect that helps pollen move from one flower to another so it can make seeds

predator an animal that hunts and eats other animals

prey an animal that is eaten by other animals

rodent one of a group of mammals that includes mice, rats, voles and squirrels

segment a section of the body

species a particular type of animal or plant

streamlined shaped so it can move easily in water or air

thorax the middle section of an insect's body

urban something which is in, or relates to, a town or city environment

vegetation another word for plants

venomous animals and plants that can release a poisonous substance, called venom, when they bite or sting

wingspan the length from the tip of one wing to the tip of another

URBAN WILDLIFE CHECKLIST

- [ ] adder, 50
- [ ] ash, 74
- [ ] badger, 43
- [ ] beech, 77
- [ ] blackbird, 18
- [ ] black garden ant, 6
- [ ] black-headed gull, 31
- [ ] bluebottle, 63
- [ ] blue tit, 17
- [ ] bramble, 80
- [ ] bream, 54
- [ ] brimstone moth, 68
- [ ] brown long-eared bat, 44
- [ ] brown mottlegill, 85

- [ ] brown rat, 39
- [ ] brown trout, 54
- [ ] buff-tailed bumblebee, 71
- [ ] buttercup, 78
- [ ] Canada goose, 25
- [ ] carrion crow, 22
- [ ] cellar spider, 59
- [ ] chaffinch, 16
- [ ] chicken of the woods, 85
- [ ] chub, 54
- [ ] cinnabar moth, 68
- [ ] collared dove, 21
- [ ] common backswimmer, 65
- [ ] common carp, 53

- [ ] common frog, 46
- [ ] common lizard, 51
- [ ] common pipistrelle, 44
- [ ] common pond skater, 65
- [ ] common puffball, 85
- [ ] common ragwort, 81
- [ ] common toad, 47
- [ ] common wasp, 71
- [ ] common woodlouse, 60
- [ ] coot, 29
- [ ] cow parsley, 81
- [ ] cranefly, 63
- [ ] daisy, 78
- [ ] dandelion, 79
- [ ] earthworm, 56

- [ ] Egyptian goose, 25
- [ ] elephant hawk-moth, 69
- [ ] emperor dragonfly, 64
- [ ] European eel, 55
- [ ] feral pigeon, 20
- [ ] fly agaric, 84
- [ ] forget-me-not, 79
- [ ] fox, 34
- [ ] garden slug, 57
- [ ] garden snail, 56
- [ ] garden spider, 58
- [ ] garden tiger moth, 69
- [ ] giant house spider, 59
- [ ] goldfinch, 17
- [ ] grass snake, 50
- [ ] great crested newt, 48
- [ ] great tit, 16
- [ ] green lacewing, 61
- [ ] grey heron, 28
- [ ] grey squirrel, 37
- [ ] gudgeon, 55
- [ ] hart's tongue fern, 83
- [ ] hawthorn, 74
- [ ] hedgehog, 45
- [ ] herb robert, 80
- [ ] herring gull, 30
- [ ] holly, 74
- [ ] holly blue, 67
- [ ] horse chestnut, 77
- [ ] housefly, 62
- [ ] house mouse, 36
- [ ] house sparrow, 14
- [ ] ivy, 82
- [ ] jackdaw, 22
- [ ] Jersey tiger moth, 68
- [ ] kestrel, 33
- [ ] kingfisher, 28
- [ ] large yellow underwing moth, 69
- [ ] lichen, 82
- [ ] London plane, 76
- [ ] long-tailed tit, 17
- [ ] magpie, 23
- [ ] male-fern, 83
- [ ] mallard, 26
- [ ] mandarin duck, 27
- [ ] marmalade hoverfly, 63
- [ ] mole, 42
- [ ] moorhen, 29

- [ ] moss, 83
- [ ] muntjac deer, 41
- [ ] mute swan, 24
- [ ] oak, 72
- [ ] orange-tip, 67
- [ ] otter, 38
- [ ] palmate newt, 49
- [ ] peacock (butterfly), 66
- [ ] peppered moth, 69
- [ ] perch, 53
- [ ] peregrine falcon, 32
- [ ] pied wagtail, 19
- [ ] pike, 52
- [ ] rabbit, 42
- [ ] red admiral, 67

- [ ] red deer, 40
- [ ] red mason bee, 70
- [ ] red squirrel, 37
- [ ] red-tailed bumblebee, 70
- [ ] ring-necked parakeet, 21
- [ ] robin, 15
- [ ] roe deer, 41
- [ ] rosebay willowherb, 80
- [ ] seven-spot ladybird, 61
- [ ] shaggy inkcap, 84
- [ ] silver birch, 74
- [ ] slow-worm, 51
- [ ] small tortoiseshell, 66

- [ ] smooth newt, 48
- [ ] sparrowhawk, 33
- [ ] starling, 23
- [ ] stinging nettle, 81
- [ ] swift, 19
- [ ] sycamore, 74
- [ ] three-spined stickleback, 55
- [ ] tufted duck, 27
- [ ] water vole, 39
- [ ] whirligig beetle, 65
- [ ] white clover, 78
- [ ] woodpigeon, 20
- [ ] wren, 15
- [ ] yellow corydalis, 79
- [ ] zebra spider, 59